Rookie Read-About® Science

It Could Still Be A Cat

By Allan Fowler

Consultants:
Robert L. Hillerich, Professor Emeritus,
Bowling Green State University, Bowling Green, Ohio
Consultant, Pinellas County Schools, Florida

Lynn Kepler, Educational Consultant

Fay Robinson, Child Development Specialist

CHILDRENS PRESS®
CHICAGO

Design by Beth Herman Design Associates

Library of Congress Cataloging-in-Publication Data

Fowler, Allan.
    It could still be a cat / by Allan Fowler.
      p. cm. –(Rookie read-about science)
    Summary: Describes the physical characteristics and behavior of cats
and examines some different kinds.
    ISBN 0-516-06015-5
    1. Cats–Juvenile literature. [1. Cats.] I. Title. II. Series: Fowler, Allan.
Rookie read-about science.
SF445.7.F68   1993
636.8–dc20   93-881
                                                CIP
                                                AC

Cats can be so quiet.

They walk on padded feet,
without making a sound.

When a cat is happy, it purrs very softly.

If a cat is living right next door, you might not even hear it.

But a cat could make a lot
of noise and still be a cat.

Have you ever heard a hungry cat meowing?

Or two cats howling in the middle of the night?

9

Some cats like to sit as still
as statues for a long time.

But a cat could jump and run
around and still be a cat –

11

especially when it's a kitten.

Kittens like to play and poke their noses into things.

Some cats enjoy being
picked up and petted.

But some cats don't.
And their feelings should
be respected.

Have you ever seen a cat licking its fur?

That's how cats keep clean.

Every cat has whiskers, and most cats have tails.

But a cat might have no tail that you can see and still be a cat, like a Manx cat.

19

Tabbies are gray, red, black, or brown, with stripes or spots.

Tortoiseshell cats have
mixed coats of black,
orange, and cream.

A Siamese cat has a light-colored coat. But its head, paws, and tail are darker.

Persian cats are white, red, or black. Or sometimes grayish-blue. Their fur is long and silky.

The cats we keep as pets
are called domestic cats.

But a cat could live in the wild and still be a cat, like a bobcat.

It could be as big and
strong as a leopard, jaguar,
or cougar and still be a cat.

Lions and tigers are the
biggest cats of all.

If you have a pet cat, make sure it has a clean litter box, plenty of cat food, and a bowl of water every day.

It will give you lots of love
in its quiet, catlike way.

Words You Know

domestic

kitten

paws

whiskers

cats

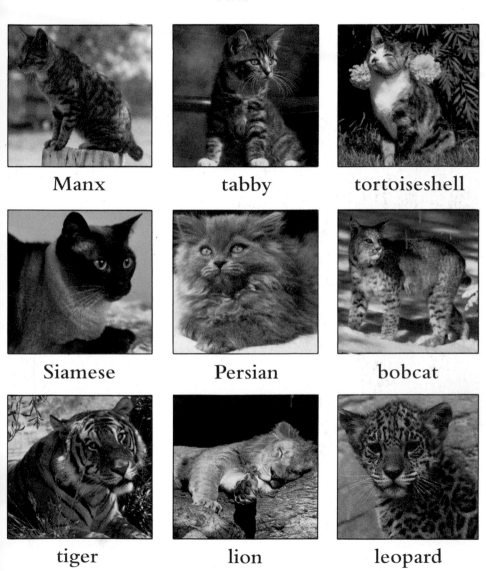

Manx

tabby

tortoiseshell

Siamese

Persian

bobcat

tiger

lion

leopard

Index

About the Author

Allan Fowler is a free-lance writer with a background in advertising. Born in New York, he lives in Chicago now and enjoys traveling.

Photo Credits

©Norvia Behling – 11, 19, 31 (top left)

SuperStock International, Inc. – 31 (bottom center); ©Gunner Kullenberg, Cover; ©Bernard Baudet, 3, 30 (bottom right); ©Tom Rosenthal, 7; ©Akira Matoba, 13, 30 (top right); ©Kris Coppieters, 20, 31 (top center); ©Mauritius, 25, 31 (center right); ©Jurg Klages, 26, 31 (bottom right); ©Mick Roessler, 27, 31 (bottom left)

Valan – ©J.R. Page, 4, 28; ©Michael J. Johnson, 5; ©Wouterloot-Gregoire, 6; ©V. Wilkinson, 9; ©Alan Wilkinson, 10, 21, 31 (top right); ©J.A. Wilkinson, 12, 23, 31 (center center); ©John Cancalosi, 14; ©Herman H. Giethoorn, 15, 22, 31 (center left); ©John Fowler, 16, 24, 30 (top left); ©Kennon cooke, 17, 29, 30 (bottom left)

COVER: Tabby Cat

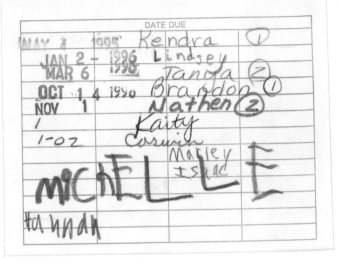

DATE DUE		
MAY 2 1995	Kendra	①
JAN 2 - 1996	Lindsey	
MAR 6 1996	Tanya	②
OCT 1 4 1996	Brandon	①
NOV 1	Nathen	②
1	Kaity	
1-02	Corwin	
	Marley	
MICHELLE	Isaac	
Hannah		

CATS

E
636.8
FOW

Fowler, Allan.

It could still be a cat.

SILVERTON SCHOOL LIBRARY